BLOOMING
FIASCOES

BLOOMING FIASCOES

POEMS

ELLEN HAGAN

TriQuarterly Books / Northwestern University Press
Evanston, Illinois

TriQuarterly Books
Northwestern University Press
www.nupress.northwestern.edu

Printed in the United States of America

10   9   8   7   6   5   4   3   2   1

Library of Congress Cataloging-in-Publication Data

Names: Hagan, Ellen, author.
Title: Blooming fiascoes : poems / Ellen Hagan.
Description: Evanston, Illinois : TriQuarterly Books/Northwestern University Press,
    2021.
Identifiers: LCCN 2020027696 | ISBN 9780810143142 (paperback) | ISBN
    9780810143159 (ebook)
Subjects: LCGFT: Poetry.
Classification: LCC PS3608.A338 B55 2021 | DDC 811/.6—dc23
LC record available at https://lccn.loc.gov/2020027696

CONTENTS

TO THE HAWK THAT CIRCLED J. HOOD PARK—

All you did was dance sky—all talon
& glide, all mesmerize. How you
arched the flow, flipped & flown. How
bravado you were, how blunt
in your boisterousness. No regard
to playground politics. All the stroll
& swing, sandbox funk of five-
year-olds—slide & roll, the pumped
legs, the way kids've got no idea
what's coming. & us either. But
somehow you pushed up. Pummel
pumped through budded trees—
You managed that rat blooming
inside your mouth. You went
for what would feed you. Quenched
all your hunger
& flew.

I AM NOT DEAD, I'M DORMANT

Sometimes you have to cut back to grow stronger
—from a sign at New York Botanical Garden

Or what is rejuvenation, renewal, revival!
Spring or sprung. Stimulant. Stimulation.
How about awaken exhilaration. Rouse
& romp. Pique. Titillate. Let me lay all
& every bone in my body. Down, down.
So I can be accelerate. Be upgrade & ascent
Boom upturn & rise. Let me improvise all
the ways to recuperate. Be regenerate. Better
off next time. Cure. Like logic. Let me illustrate
my comeback. Call it revivification if you will.
Say quickening & watch me come. Holler
awaken & watch me phoenix or wolf better
more like it. Just the way you like it. *Not.* Ha!
Let me consolidate. My potentiality is precious
& it's a flourish of efflorescence. A flowering
eruption if you will. That's what I'm up to.
In case you were wondering why I hadn't
& don't plan to. Return your call. Or email.
Or any of the other bullshit. *Damn!* Let me rest.
So I can stand back up in my full-on blossoming.

I

or begins. Is hieroglyph of vagina. Every entry that opens is a door. Is a bar
full of medicine & herbs or what heals. Exists. No exits. A thruway. Hallway.
All the temperate regions, each temperature, or what it means to be curious.
Curiosity like a luck—locket, some charm or stone or gold I can wear,
costume or dress in. Take off & on. Sometimes I get the feeling of traveling
the planet. Some. Times I want to stay directly. Perfectly still. Dichotomous.
Branching. My axis. Access. Versatile. Voracious. I have all the time been
orange. Not violent necessarily, but not—not violent. Scars & such.

II

I haven't lived as hard as I used to, but not to say my life is soft now. It's not.
Not a day goes by that I don't see a bird or a rat crushed clear through, their
existence shot, full-on feathers and guts, internalized, at every crosswalk.
Every day I lead the two hearts & rib cages I created inside my whole
body, across carcasses & bloated condoms, over dog shit endless & people
sometimes praising God or their idea of God near the Children's Place on
microphones and loaded sound systems. I hold their hands—the ones that
grew in my womb & we pass disaster, dirt & trash & the men's homeless
shelter & the new bones of buildings & people finding & ending their highs
near the bus terminal. There is no fresh shelter I've crafted around us. I have
not—don't think—chosen the easy way. A journey marked with any answers
or cleanliness you might choose if you were say—a blue or a green or some
color more accustomed to peace or calm. I remain unchanged. Most of
me still as reckless as when I entered the world shooting straight from my
mother's holy bloody canal.

Or what it means to land
or space or matter or the length
of goodbye. Or I miss you. Or when
will you return? Oh mothering. Oh trajectory.
Oh landscape & time. Oh light that keeps stretching
oh sky & guilt. Oh sex & disaster. Oh keeping you alive.
Oh breath & time. Oh sponge of muscle. Oh the way you grip.
Oh grit. & pleasure. Oh sunlight & plants & oxygen. Oh swing set
on a night of sunsets & planets. Oh planet of my lungs & hearts.
Oh blanket of blessings & palm trees & caffeine & lust & head lice
& all the ways to say I'm needy & I'm needing. & I need you. & I'm lost
& there's more world than even you can imagine. & it's all there—waiting.

GATES OPEN—

When an infant emerges
womb to world. Soft
& susceptible. Their gums
enter packed to the gills.

Molars & molars, canines
& lateral & central incisors
they arrive primed to rip
& gnaw. Their mouths

full for the blooming.
Enamel encapsulating
calcium & phosphate
pulp & dentin, cementum

& membrane. All blood
supply & nerve. Tissue
alight & alive inside
their small cavernous maws.

So when my youngest loses
her first tooth. Pulls it up
a bouquet of blood floods
her lips a crooked red smile.

How adult she suddenly is.
Flush & gaping. An atrium
inside of her. *I feel teenaged*
she says. My own jaw aching

a tender trench inside of me.
As I watch her shed & slip
from one whole body
into another.

ONCE

I, too, was a girl with a fresh mouth
& gums loaded with teeth
that would all fall out.

Now Miriam. Hip jutted
at the sink. Spillage.
A glut of blood.
How each year
is marked
by what we lose
what is lost
how to say
goodbye.

Alarm! Alarm!
Whole mouthed
alarm! She cries
a hollering
farewell.
You tooth
served me well.
How you marked me
held on
until I was ready
to crack loose
without out.

ITEMIZATION—PART I

What luxury—start
    to consider the letdown
        the breasts & their heave.

Body remembers
    spearmint cigarette tongue thrust
        screeching towards thirteen.

The body forgets
    hymen unhinged all teenaged
        game shows as background.

But sure remembers
    the buckling tremble of want
        all erupting song.

& recognizes
    how ocean it can become
        in his nimble hands.

& yes witnesses
    what a decade can reveal
        all swallow & crave.

ITEMIZATION—PART II

for my mom, Gianina Bazaz, & her father, Aziz Bazaz

Memorize the nose
cliff dive, then jump stunt of it
Gianina—Aziz

Aziz as cherished
meaning beloved, fisherman
tailor of men's suits

5 a.m. wake up
Aziz of salt, shrimp cocktail
man of fins & thread.

See his flaunt of nose
each nostril a promenade
how brazen & proud.

Gianina as grace
third daughter, his browned skin twin
Assyrian girl.

Gianina as luck
look, her mint leaves & kabob
girl of clever swim.

See her sexy snout
bodacious beak bellowing
adore her muzzle.

& glorify yours
marvel your snooty charmer
sniff the planet gold.

NURSE

for Miriam & the months of moonlit feedings

What it means to feed—cure pits of hunger
in the belly of the newest girl—occupy weight.

To quench & round cheeks, heft thighs, increase
all the body. Train the tongue to be swallow.

Know satiety, not rumble or be—moan. Teach
the technicalities, mechanics of mouth—manipulate

maneuver the milk—pomegranate   gold   hurricane
nutrient & red flow wonder wine & whined whoa—

peak to nourish all of your 17 pounds, hold & ply
you with ocean river over—flow salt—all

the rush. All the sweet. All that is yours—of me.

TO THE DREAMS THAT MADE ME SEARCH—

In those early days & weeks, when her body still
felt latched & attached to all of me. & my body

was a waste of hormones dreading the bed each night.
Night sweats. Night terrors. A season of ocean. A king

sized river each dawn. All of me salt. All of me a wave
of surrender. The dreams came fraught & fought me alert.

Where's the baby? Where's her body? Where's she hiding?
Beneath? Below? Still inside? Not delivered? Not removed?

But—a drunken search through sheets to find her.
Every night of those weeks I would dream her lost to me.

Me suffocater. Me drowner or loser of all things
once connected by umbilical cord. & then I'd wake

& there she'd be—asleep beside me & later asleep
in her crib down the hall & now asleep in her own bed.

All of her, arms flung at night—readying her own dreams.
& each day I'm leaving who she is reckless in the world.

How she'll ride buses & trains, enter airport security, do dance moves well
or not, first kiss, jumble her own language, how she already hopscotches
& Hula-Hoops without me. How she already spells the names of all her
friends. How she dots the *i* in her name when I'm not around. How whole &
wilderness she'll be—how escape & meander. How grateful I'll be knowing
all the times I found her safe & warm & right exactly where I left her.

TO RAISE YOU, DAUGHTER

So you have enough breath to keep from
drowning. Limbs to swim, teach treading,
wailing below water, to swallow sea if urgent.

Mark Mississippi, Ohio & Hudson too, birth
seagulls on the Grand Concourse, any thing
extraordinary for mapping, direction, familiar.

For the sake of living things. You should know
how to grow tails & wings & triple tongues, teeth
& extra legs for outrunning, leap, for escape.

If you have to be dragon, so be it. Cyclops too
& Loch Ness, Bigfoot's flexing counterpart, part
mermaid, lobster girl, medusa, fantasy, fiction

child. If you have to morph magic—I hope
I've taught you well—& how.

MIRIAM

after Mamaw

How you were born ancestor. Arrived sectioned from me.
Abdomen & what it means to be gutted. Both fists knotted
knees to chest—sometimes blood can be blessing. You
already knew how to holler. How roughhouse outside me,

how country. & all of you after my own Mamaw, who was
small & subdued. Docile—who bore nine children & lost two—
swam barefoot in rivers, made skillet-fried cornbread that made
me weep when she left. Her ghosted body re-arriving through mine.

Origin storied from uterus to crib. We named you knowing.
Miriam—meaning bitter or rebellious, meaning strong waters / river
beds, banks & what the tides could merge, re-immerge. Named you
for her.

So when you—smallest Miriam—cling to the neck of my father,
who was my Mamaw's oldest & most beloved, & when you say love
cradled in his arms—we know death is only a smallest exhale,
a transformation from one set of lungs to another.

How much it takes to love the smallest bodies outside of yours,
or what it means to cradle distance, or when you wake in your bed
I wake in mine. Us two all the time linked. When there you are
all I know of home. Walking away from me.

SELF-PORTRAIT AT 36 WITH DAVID

Barnegat Light, New Jersey—April 4, 2015

Because looking at myself without you beside me is unnatural
& though *the light is all wrong*—your camera slung & up

the light feels right to me, warm & soft, your chest pressed
against my back, both our heads angling up, up at the dock,

boat slips on the bay—all the scallops secure in the sea still,
their bone-less bodies soft. & our own getting softer each day.

Sometimes the mirror makes our features fun-house style
& we're way more old age than the teen age we most times feel,

or the slight of shutter promises supple & smooth, where edge
& ravine & straight-up wrinkle have arrived & settled in

like vulnerable houseguests we don't have the heart to kick out.
How comfortable they've become all over our fine faces

& my neck—how they've become familiar with our privacy. How
we've begun to cradle them. Stitch & loom. In the photograph

there we are—chins tilted just next to one another, mouths closed

& turned up. A type of satisfaction dead in this middle we're both in.

TO THE PERIOD STILL ARRIVING & MARKING THE WHOLE OF ME—

It's not the blood, it's the gore, way

the back bend / breaks

    cycle

        tide

under wind / wind / winded.

The way the blood is a blossom,

    the basin marked with blooming.

My body a crew of noise.

An electric surrender.

Erotic & dousing everything I touch.

It's not the gore, it's the blood.

    & it's everywhere

I want it to be.

TO 3:47 A.M. WHEN YOUR YOUNGEST THROWS UP IN HER BED—

by god you think & plunge your hand towards her sheets
while your husband whispers—*why would you touch it?*
Footsie pajama bodied shiver, she plunges her all at you—

You, hold the vomit towards God (the capital one this time)
& curse *fuck* & loud *(god/God) damn it.* & your oldest peeks
awake, says—*can we wake now? How's 'bout a movie?* How's

about we hold here on the rug, cuddle close 'cause it's 3:52 a.m.
now & the cold's keeping outside & the hot water's running
& every need of every want keeps on getting met, my God.

Thank the bodies & the way they dispel. Thank the expanding
of each lung, & how we all sometimes heave towards daylight.
Thank daylight too & electricity & the astounding capacity
of luck that leaves you weeping into morning—

NONE OF IT FOR GRANTED—

Not their still small bodies rushing the bed—overflow
what weight they carry heavy atop me.

Or Miriam's curled hair a wash of sleep & matte
a piling of breath & sucked morning air.

Not the overflowing coffeepot, churned almond butter
panella & poached eggs. Not their endless

hunger. Or mine. Not the A train puncturing uptown
collecting our buoy of limbs. No,

not Central Park in an April sky so cold our down
coats bolster our bodies—still. Still

the sun is intoxicate & cleanse, all high & warm
when we need it, so no,

not the neon yellow Virgin Mary in the sculpture
garden or David Bowie & the girls

their two heads shaking on the monitors at MoMA
& not even Miri run, running

rushing the fountain at full speed could make me
take it for granted. Granted,

these days are not always easy. & sometimes it takes
all that's in me to get from one moment

to the next without feeling a waste of exhaust & *fuck it*,
but today, all of me is a debt of bows

to all the things I will not take for granted, no,
not David in the kitchen, podcast blast on Sundays

when the week doesn't feel crushing or already too
much, or oh god how can I get from here to—

No, not baked salmon with shallot & brussels sprouts,
or the parmesan on your rice.

& not the pile of stories or Celi's new words she reads
aloud & her book *Sex Is a Funny*

Word & we both laugh because it is & we both get
the joke. & the beds are all warm.

& all of us curled double time into each other. No,
not one second for granted.

PICTURE THIS

for Miriam Dawson Hagan, or Mamaw & her wildest woman self

If it's the last pink salad syrupy sweet that you'll eat
cooled whip, coconut & walnuts & the last stuffing sliced
with onions in their thin skins—sage & salt. If it's the last
& it is—cornmeal fried to bread—go ahead & relish.

Remind your gullet to savor New Haven's winding roads
& the goats in yards & the blindfolded wheelbarrow game.
Papaw calling porch rules & seven aunts & uncles & sixteen cousins
with all their legs & bodies stained with grass, their raucous laughs.

See Miriam Dawson Hagan as she was—not at the end—littered
breath, uterus falling—all the children weighing her smallest
body down, down. & the one they lost—ninth—& Uncle Joe
whose bulbous lungs became ocean & his body floated away.

Years chiseling skin to dust, her humped spine—curved, curling.
Don't see the fade, or the slow motion. See her still weekly hairdo
bouncing with its curl & the corsage of carnations at her breastbone. See
her ripe, wily, pouring grease into skillets, frying, her lap, apron slung.

See her down the river—bathing suit, cap & your own fish of a mother—
warning you of snakes, the deep end, all the fish & fins & teeth, warning
you of New Haven & its country ways & *who swims in rivers after all?*

Now see your mamaw as she was—swimming—smile like a dare,
with her bare, young legs, toes flirting with crawdads—watch her sly,
study her quick—tendons, muscles, all, in.

WATCHING LOVE—

& how it swims across the bay. Dunks
& cannonballs. Holds its breath. Drinks
bourbon on the porch. Listens slow
to the ocean's swell & calm. Love
sorting rocks with the girls in the yard.
Love ordering a whole Italian hoagie
with onions, oil & vinegar & you name it,
salami, mortadella. Love sitting to watch
cartoons with its sweet sugary breath.
Love making morning coffee hot
when you rise. Love catching waves
& sand crabs & one full-on crab
with pinchers to the sky. You all yelp
at love. How brazen, how unafraid.
Love takes outside showers still
in September. Devours Grandma pie
& Popeye's on the road home.
Love falls fast asleep in the backseat
after food & holding & kisses
back rubs & rowdy laughter. Such luck
to know love so well. Riding shotgun
with you. Right up until the end.

MIRIAM DAWSON HAGAN

You skillet sizzler woman, grease eyed pop
& hot, you stove chanter, apron wearer,
corn bread slayer.

Knife wielder, waist shaker, you witchy kitchen
woman of coven & craft. You palm swatter,
shift slinger, corn boiler.

Late stayer, crossword doer, milk drinker, country-
fied, sweet spot haver, arms plenty, hand
wringer.

You stuffing wizard, veggie chopper, spin winner,
potato skinner, lard user, slim sister
oven runner.

You spatula wielder, casserole baker, butter
to his bread, you tall tale teller, turkey dresser,
sous chef shit talker.

You exalted sweet tea mixer, fried egg wonder,
majestic Mama to nine bodies, you grand-
grander. Show stunner,

all the time. I miss you.

My father sitting cross-legged on the steps of the seashore having the smallest tea party with my smallest daughter. He is different than he was before. & last night—the story he told me about Leo Spalding. His best friend from New Haven, Kentucky, who died in the car ride home from their first day at community college. How they were rowdy 18-year-old country boys—first generation to go. How my dad tells it he convinced Leo to go with him, rather than sell cars & pinball machines like Leo's daddy did. *Something better*, my dad said. & when the car ran off the road, my dad survived with 35 stitches & he didn't know Leo'd died until he woke up in the hospital the next morning. How in those days, the ambulances were hearses. *I didn't know anything about PTSD then, or therapy, or how I'd blamed myself the whole time. How maybe Leo'd been better off—*

You say moonshine, illegal, the boot's only leg—low down
unauthorized, unhinged & loose. You say moon, shined
hell broke & break (ed) loose. Rowdy bawdy. Midnight rise,
moon & still distilled. Liquor & licensed, licensed
to rise, spirit to shine, burn the oak & white lightning fine.
You say unaged & heirloom, punctuate & proof, you call
it hooch, honey mountain dew, sweet smuggled swig.

Makes me see Kentucky, Appalachian mountain mayhem
makes me see myself at 13 & beyond. & yeah, you coulda
called me all that—swill & free, illicit whiskey woman, all
sugar sweet—go 'head pour me in the spoon. Watch me
catch fire.

SAME

It's not the first
  & won't be the last
   fight with your daughter
    how she'll wail, whine & want
     all the things she can't have. To
      stay later & love longer & sugar
       high. How she'll cry & wander on
        pretend you don't exist, throw you
         all off-balance & trust you can't keep
          up with her & she's right. Little, little you
           existing exactly the way you did just years
            before. Doing whatever the hell she wants
             & smiling in your face while she does it. Whew
              you go on & deep breath & meditate & breathe out
               make believe she's got nothing on you, while you fake
               wave at your neighbors & hope they don't hear you quiet
               shout for her to *listen to me. Please*, you say, even quieter.
              You know for certain begging never worked with you, but
              sometimes it's late & you're all out of options & when she
              asks you to take her suitcase down—says she's planning to live
              outside. Alone. You both can't help but get tickled at the request
              & instead of weeping, you both laugh, seeing just how twin you really are.

TO THE BREASTS WHEN IT'S OVER—

You two heave heavies, glory rockers
right-on drop gold rum bumpers.

Didn't you divine & dine, feed &
fortify—you heavened helpers, plenty

planters, mystifiers mag-fucking-nificent
the fact you fed for five years & now.

You make me mourn & moan, make
merry with *it's over*. Sure the baby

still needing nighttime nursing, you
dwindle to dribble. Infant to toddler

god (damn) soon enough these girls
will be *those girls* as you watch them

walkrunjumpdanceplaypunksneakdive
away from you. But you won't forget

there was a time when all their hunger
was quenched. By you.

WHAT WE DO—NOW

after Gwendolyn Brooks

We mourn, we bless,
we blow, we wail, we
wind—down, we sip,
we spin, we blind, we
bend, bow & hem. We
hip, we blend, we bind,
we shake, we shine,
shine. We lips & we
teeth, we praise & protest.
We document & we
drama. We demand &
we flow, fold & hang
loose. We measure &
we moan, mourn & whine
low. & we live & we
breathe. & some of the time,
we don't.

Tonight, I am here. Here
& tired. Here & awake,
sure, & alive. Yes here &
still, still here, still & here
& still awake & still still
alive.

AS IF OVERNIGHT—

The city has sprung alive

blooming fiasco
blooming resilience
blooming disaster
blooming hyacinth
blooming asbestos
blooming electric
blooming traffic jams
blooming flowered trees
blooming rising seas
blooming bird & flight
blooming resistance
blooming ice cream trucks
blooming stomach bugs
blooming bicycles
blooming playground drama
blooming sweaty pits
blooming downward dog
blooming April sun
blooming songs & ways
to sing them.

TELL ME ALL THE THINGS YOU'D MISS—

If you're asleep—note—if you're not awake,
wide eyes, you could miss—there is much.

The hefty rat, its rot, right eye, steady steel
& gray body upturned & turned in on itself,
the glue trap's coffin & concrete grave
on Audubon's quietest 8:20 a.m. street. Just
face & tail taunting world. Avert her eyes,

or try, but she'll look anyway because she is
awake, alert, still. Her—*can we take the rat back
into nature?* As in: this is not, but in a way, it is.
& you'd miss the second rat—run over by bike,

black cab, stroller, wheelie, BMX, skateboard,
its mangled body bruised, bashed, but tail still
& intact. You'd miss the used tampon, its bloody
animal arrival on 177th Street blocking the A train's

elevated entrance. Distance's only cousin—huddle.
& the body of the woman. Uterus's shunt & stroll,
heave of the hips & her heft. Or the scattering
of white rice everywhere from Broadway to St. Nick
to Amsterdam—all their holy grains, how they rose

up like the smallest baptisms, miniature prayers
filling the streets with a kind of voracious, simple

yearning.

TO THE SLEEPING WOMAN IN CINDY'S BAKERY ON THE CORNER OF ST. NICHOLAS & 179TH ST.

Who hasn't dream | dreamed of falling asleep
to the smell of bread. Baking. All that oven
all that heat all that yeast sharing city space.
Who hasn't argued with their bones

told them it's time to take a seat—said
hey femur hello collarbone won't you stop a spell
put the body down | down.
How hunger can wreck the gut—make us ravage | ravaged.

How hunger becomes hammer | exhaustion
the light that never changes | how it tolls
& clangs—how a stomach surrenders, how you
slept amidst café con leche, donuts crammed with sugar,

between the bustle hectic | the morning grind
the—*gotta get there in time* | you paused the whole
morning | erased rush. You said *I'm too done to move*
on this March Thursday.

Ghosted hands holding each other. Stink of leavening
the silent | still of her mouth. Head heavy
& all that rising | rising behind her | a fury
of what it means to gratify.

SOAKED MOURNING

That this spring has been
trauma is not a fucking joke.

Misted rain, missed trains
matched caps to rain jackets.

City spun with un-ripened
buds shunted to trees, timid.

Months of waiting, days dying
when I read you—news you un-

ravel the gore & insides of me.
Us, bussed to home & families, jobs

& each hustled day. Pick up any
paper or feed—see the mouths

all the mothers & their empty arms
see the frames of our children.

The way we all wait for some reck-
oning—some way to navigate how

bullets bury in skin, the way hate
is a plume, feathers & flaunt all

choked & ravaging, blistered, burn-
ishing—a hot, blooming wreckage.

TO THE WOMAN ON ST. NICHOLAS AVENUE WHOSE THIGH WAS A WILDERNESS BLOOMING—

There you sat, gardenias & fat lemon trees bursting forth
from what appeared to be vulva—very near uppermost thigh.
That place we all of us blossom out from. You with all
your gnarled pinkest roses streaming upwards, all froth & funk
from the newspaper stand—none of it could contain
the many multitudes shooting forth from your thigh, how
it was full of satsumas & mangoes alike, sweet syrup of the streets.

All of you looked ragged & ravaged & I'm not one to judge, as much
of me looks the same so much of the time. & none of us immune to
tolls the days take & all of us whole reveling in the days given.
But my God—what contrast was your knee to your hip, what bright hot
youth. How a body part can so quickly become avocado tree, magnolia,
peony, the way one opens up like sex, the way a clitoris swells
& swolls, how deep & divine a leg can look all draped over workhorse
right there in the middle stench/steam of city living.

Look, I want to say, look at this woman with her whole billowing self
(even as the rest of her is fading). All that ink on all that skin. God,
what a garden of a woman. What catapult, what precision. All,
all of her springing outward & alive.

TO THE CONDOM ON 167TH STREET SPRAWLED
BETWEEN FINDLAY & COLLEGE AVENUES

just steps from the Bronx Writing Academy & down
a stretch from Grand Concourse Jamaican Bakery. You
aren't at all pompous in the way you lay, spent & breath
less, all the life (force) spilled from you onto sidewalk. Sex,
like some public promenade & why not? *Jesus.* Sex alive & not
petrified or pious. Maybe promiscuous, but protective too, so
what—sex on the street, awake & in person. No shame.
Condom—how you carried no weight, just empty funk, all
of you splayed in supplication. Craving certainty. It's a Thursday

& I channel slow jams like an ovulation playlist, and you
show up as if rising from the city & its grind
of sludge. Its daily meditation on trash & the way its stench
surges & the existence of water bugs & their collective hard shells,
as if un-earth-ing (along with dust & mice & shit) a pleasure principle,
a pulse, cry out, a moment of pause & straight *fuck* in all the catastrophe
city life allows, a moment of *hallelujah* & *oh yes* & *right there.* Some
times sex is dirty. It's OK to ask for it.

On the BX 35, who isn't dreaming of their own bodies billowing
& straight coming into atmosphere. Who isn't imagining their own
lumbering & young young or old old bodies being worship-adored,
undeniably wanted. What construction worker, social worker, teacher,
headed to school next week isn't daydreaming about what wetness
wreaks on a body & what want manages to unwrap from skin? Thrust
of nothingness, obliterate. Who isn't imagining the small death of orgasm—
always?

So much of the time we spend clothed, our own breasts & thighs wrapped so snug against all the elemental-ness. Our whole sheaves cloistered on trains & in cars, at desks hunched & pitiful, so many hours of so many days un-touched even when in love—so much time protected from the simple act of love, that to see you sweet, gullible, vulnerable condom—to see you splayed out on 167th Street is to feel a whole city's collective sigh & feel all the flush you bring when we sure need it most.

TO THE WOMAN FALLING TO SLEEP BESIDE ME—

It's more than exhaust. I'm sure
her shoulders slumped. Slipping
to abyss or absence. Obliterate.

Don't want her to concuss. Slight
or blink. I pretend ignorance. No
sense of personal space. bumpslide

nudgegroovepushshovewakewake
upupupupupupupupupupupupupup
Bus can make you sleep. Surrender

is what I say. *Come on. Let's talk.*
How long it's been since I've been
this close. To letting go myself.

EXPRESS TO WORK

Because your body smells of sweat, sawdust,
9–5 & lemon rind. Smells of coffee grinds & time.

How polite your skin is against mine. *NY Times*
& this. Daily grind. Grind. Crime in times. News

& crime. Grind & time. Time & grind. Warnings
never end & it's cold—keep a coat on & it's bustle

graffiti, train track trance—all of us a spell. Scarf
the neck, close the collar, cross the legs, tilt the head,

heed the call, catch the ride. Home—it's always home.
Steel the grin, watch the back, break the spell, bind

the cap, keep the eyes. Awake the call. Cast the grind.
Carry home.

Ekphrastic poem based on the painting
Untitled by Maxwell Taylor

TO THE BROKEN MATTRESS ON PARK AVENUE & 167TH IN THE BRONX—

You cradle all the resting bodies, allow sleep & glow
you heavy with memory, weight & let go.

What sighs you must carry—what linger
swollen vowels & layered heat.

Baby, said soft & syrupy, *baby, baby*. Oh!
All the times you've nursed & nestled.

Every second hauled & held. All of you
springs & buoy. Catch & carry. Maintain

the every day. Place of hibernate & slow down
drowse & deep sigh. You carrier of yawn & nod.

Wonder at how you've swayed the stress of each waking.
Lullabied or crooned someone to sleep or drift away.

How you've eased the heavy of dreams—all the lives
you've carried along each night—reaching morning.

TO THE SHARK FIN ON THE BULLET TRAIN FROM
SENDAI TO TOKYO—

How ocean you are. How deep dark sea scrawl,
belly crawl how you taste of raw & helpless, how you lapse

& drape, thwap the whole of your boneless accordion
around my tongue. How you sidle & meander rock

loose & let flap. How you must have held memory,
a rollicking jut of salt & sand. The waves' buoyant frolic

towards hunger & then sate.

How you never expected the hook,

all you knew then was swim. Eat or get eaten.
& all the time I am thinking that those of us on land
are doing the exact
same thing.

SHELTER

Because staying dry is sometimes   remedy
all those metal spokes jutting about
plastic handle hold on tight.   Canopy
awning from sky   arcing from down
pour.   Because there was no rain
but you held on to that smallest roof
in any case.   Coat buttoned   & styled
half relaxing on your open
half smile.   Sometimes
just the thought of protection is enough.

Ekphrastic poem from *Young Girl with Umbrella on Centre
Street Hill District, Pittsburgh 1951*, Richard Saunders

TO ESMERELY AT CLAIRE'S, WHO TELLS MY DAUGHTERS IT WON'T HURT—

Look, it always hurts. In this hell, my eyes burn cherry red fusion lemon lime explosion sea of Shopkin honey bun clip-on bubble gum soda pop purple rainbow eye shadow lip gloss blush brush unicorn tie-dye diamond crusted crustaceans on necklaces scarves that shimmer shine. The whole shebang outrageous girlish coquettish. Don't my daughters love it here. Like a sparkling beacon lighthouse ship in the distance buoy lifeboat savior. Jesus don't they anchor towards glitter? Don't they run bump awkward dance childlike hip shake at the sounds of pop culture raining down streamers of tutus and gloves with emojis? *Getting your ears pierced*—no matter the earring—be it emerald blue birthstone star lemon drop cross for Christ gold ball *is gonna hurt*. & so when Miriam—brave as she is—& she is—says she wants it done, of course I say yes. & when she smiles from heart necklaces to best friend lockets and holds on tight, I can see her whole three-and-a-half-year-old self grow eons before me. Once done, her wail is one for the ages. A heave & push. & when Miriam refuses the second ear & weeps so hard she vomits all over my scarf & coat & bag & the coats of theirs that I'm carrying, all I can think to say is *It fucking hurts, Esmerely*. And maybe one of us should have been gutsy enough to tell the truth.

TELL ME ALL THE THINGS YOU'D MISS

The man crouched beneath the Chase bank on St. Nicolas & 181st—
beneath all the money/green/wealth/ducats/bills/bets
in this great greedy city. Wearing a gray faux Mohawk
cap & a full-on hombre wig beneath—all golden breath
above & midnight curls below. His sputtering spewing
bravado with all that sexy glory. Half man | half
superstar. Half resting, half on the way to his next gig.
Chance & debutante all rolled into one. This.
You would miss.

& the layers of crabs in the truck bed—their bodies
hankering & pulling atop one another. Pink & dull.
Ready for the devouring. For whatever hunger
is about to take their breath & eat it whole.

& the A train wonder—singing backup falsetto for the band
that doesn't exist—his urine a stream of goodwill,
an underground ambassador of satisfaction. Shake & roll,
baby. Let it flow.

& the boy—his mother rushing his shoulder
& his small penis flagging in the January morning.
It's school & full bladder, cross the street, full bladder,
hail the cab, jut the walk, trip the curb hold on.
& this morning, he becomes an ocean on the platform.
Is the Hudson, all the ice melting—slosh & glow.
You would miss all this.
Sweet relief.

An opening up of—burst forth.
Froth & radiate. A palette of gold wings
or what it means to fly. A magnificent
trundle of wolves dressed as children
on my walk from Amsterdam Avenue.
Coco helado trucks that jingle a prayer
of flavored ice. Coconut & papaya.
The way an avocado peels awake. Smooth
as the huskies that live next to the taco truck
on 182nd. The way they stop me to smell the life
& sweat on my skin. How they seem to know
if I've drenched the afternoon. Animal & pleasure.
A coat of wet. Here's to the rain that washes
in droves. & the bus a miracle of pigeons
stopping to capture whole bodies
on their ways away. Blessing.
Oh flourish. Oh prayer.
Oh simple. Oh bodies.
Oh sing.

ALLOW ME

I feel full on gravity. Float. Unadjusted.
Unaccustomed. Raid style showoff. Stunted
& stunting. If I must. Say foundational. Some-
times I mother gold & the world & you & your
lost tooth & empty gums. Showoff. I shake
your accustomed foundations. Foundational.
Loose the chaos of your shift. Shit. I'm 40
& was born yesterday & today & will be again
I'm sure. Tomorrow. Each November I'm Earth.
Each revolve a record. I mark time & your skin
with my scent. I'm a tincture. To be dropped
all essential oiled like. I'm country. How many
times do I need to say it for you to believe me?
Electric shock to your system. All the words.
A hive. A system. Electronic. A code you cannot
remember. But every time you punch it in. *Oh!*
It's right there—right at the tip-top of brain.
Matter. Like memory, I show up. Showoff.

THE MEDITATION

Jersey Shore, April 2018

What's salt anyway
healing properties that wash
winter's brutal funk,

frolic that lasted
long enough to hold us close
'gainst the elements,

it's elemental.
How much all of me loves you,
watching you watch life.

The little unknowns
all that lives beneath the sea
every ruptured wave.

Sun's first subtle warmth
as our daughters play ahead
holding every breath.

Distance feels so close
how forever goes this fast,
rummaging ahead.

DIRECTIONS FOR THAT SWIM YOU KNOW YOU WANT TO TAKE—

Can't stop to
lungs jumbled, breath
out of—knocked loose from
peeled out of—fish, girl
sea, plankton, weed-

ed, way we rode, free
styled slid through, thickened hold
surfed—weightless amble
of salted sea—

don't wanna come up for—stay
underneath of, near suffoca-
tion, dunked below, sound
less—could be anemone, horse's
shoe, jelly, both wings of gulls
hampering near—sky

want to keep all limbs from
rising up, want to tread & butter
fly & stroke through, want to
train below, become buoyant.

TO THE RUBBER BAND HOLDING MY JEANS TOGETHER—

OK, it's not a real rubber band
it's a child's scrunchie
that some after-school teacher
put in Miriam's hair months ago.

& when I send the evidence to Ara
we laugh & laugh & laugh.

Because 40
Because mothering
Because bloat
Because beer
Because I like cream in my coffee
Because egg & cheese sandwiches
Because butter
Because rocky road
Because tacos
Because lasagna
Because curry
Because thick steaming bowls of ramen
Because food is love

& family & communion & breath & life & delicious & hearty & gives me heart

& this year. I do not keto or intermittent fast. I eat & love hard & ride & & &
plan to buy a bigger size pair of jeans when I can find the time. & expand a bit.
& who cares & go on & honor the body I've got. The one that holds & nurtures.
The one Miriam says she loves & squishes in all the right places & Celi who holds
my hand in hers & strokes my stomach. The one that expanded for her & I release
all the breath inside me & let go.

TONIGHT, OVULATION REIGNS—

& I send David to get ice cream & maybe cereal,
the sugary kind—the kind I don't keep in the house,
but I'm hungry for anything addictive that mimes
want in the body. How it's possible to still have eggs,
growing & cultivating in one of my ovaries. Then
their slippery release & push down the fallopian tube.
Once in a while this mystical maturity, this thickened
uterus inside of me. Is too much to bear. & I buck about
slurping down sweetness. Drinking too much. Irrational-
izing everything in my path. Destructive like & unyielding.
Feeling all centauride-ish, half human, half bucking horse
below. Something real reckless & animal inside me.

ON HEARING IN MIDDLE SCHOOL THAT A PUSSY
SMELLS LIKE FISH—

How I wish I'd said, yes I'm a saline marinade. We all are. My pussy is an avalanche
of salt. Tastes all mermaidlike & alkaline. Brine flavored. I'm savory sodium chloride.

Oceanic to the tongue. Relish the zest of my fresh, brackish flesh, I'm all surf water's
savory smack. I can sink you with my sapidity. Hook & net. Bait you with my relished

tang. My composition is compulsory, a soluble stimulus that your 7th grade self
can't contain. You think you're so cute. With what you imagine to be slant/put-down

punishment. How you lopped our sexuality down with one slight, sneering snub.
Suppression in the form of snide. How even then I imagined it compliment. Knowing

I'd find someone to long for my pungent delectability. Went to sleep secure that either way,
I loved the savorous, scrumptious sea that lived inside of me.

CARRIED AWAY

Bless the muscle inside this body.
Bless each tendon & sway.
Bless the prowess of my uterus
how it expands & expands. Galaxy
inside of me. Bless the vulva & length
of clitoris. How they'll continuously tell us
how small & compact they think we are.
How we'll stay growing. Stay expanding.
An arc inside of me. Bless the muscle.
How it juts & croons. Bless the hair—
protection from & against. Great fur of my body.
Smell & shine. Bless the vaginal canal. Entry-
way, highway, surrender, vantage point,
smuggling happiness. Bless the body's
blood. Even in its exit—holy. & alive.
The animal of my body. The muscular
comfort. Period. Bless it. Bless orgasms,
the body's exhaustion. G-spot chant call
& respond. Bless sweetness. Bless sex.
Positivity. Positively. Bless the wash of yes.
Bless the wolf inside my body. The tinged
cackle inside. The river. The tides. The salt.

All of it

bless.

TO BOTH GIRLS DIPPING BREAD IN BOWLS OF SAVORY BLACK BEANS IN THE CONDESA—

Mexico City, April 2019

You two are such earth girls. How you meander
every street. Ashore. Asunder. How you bend
& flow. How you occupy space & don't fold. Flail
your all bodies to & away. Every city you love. You
walk unafraid. Unencumbered still. Still girls. Still
so much of your lives to come. Hoping. Hoping.
You carve an open wound in me. To watch you
saunter, taste the world. Frolic & last. It's to see
you about to be grown. Up. & as much
as I love, love it. It breaks all of me apart. Too.

ADVICE TO MYSELF AFTER MY MAMMOGRAM & YEARLY DOCTOR VISIT—

Thank each day—a gift
closer now to 42
in Year of the Rat

howl at the wolf moon
bless the horse inside of me
not trotting along

full speed reckless now
no one's sure how much time's left
gonna use mine up

all & every way.

WHAT WARMS YOU MOST

When I stay up past midnight
reading about the globe & its
hothothothothothothothothot-
ness, I do not weep, or bellow
into the polluted night sky.

But do I breathe in that glorious
exhaust? Yes. Do I sleep huddled
in a kind of terrific fear? Sure. Do
I wake again in the morning? All
the time before the alarm now?
Every day ready, ready, ready,
ready, ready. My anxiety close
& comfortable. I do say yes. I do

not pray, but I do wear amazonite
around my neck like some prayer
or luck. A locket. I do not scare
easily, & so I barrel through, ride
the train, into the nightmare I keep
on reading about. Hug the people

I love most. Open my home. Invite
everyone over. Wine & chocolate
& will you sit a spell? & will you dance
until you sweat through your underwear?
& will you kiss the base of my throat
until it opens? A splay of wings riding
the shotgun of my love. I will love, love,
love, love, love, love, love, love. Love

WHEN MY FATHER CALLS

to say he has rubbed my mom's legs
for over an hour & she's resting,
it puts me at ease. Knowing she will
travel soon back to her own mother,
my grandma
who is 101 now. Strong
willed & still full. Her life a flare of yes.
All of me is grateful. & to know & love
my own mother at 71. Her mended heart
still beating, pumping, thrive, thriving.
She is an ocean & she is all the salt
in all the seas & so bold too
& knows how
to get from here to there & knows
how to teach me what it means to exist.
& knows how to cradle her mother
at the exact same time. She is thread
& mend too. Lifting & holding us all
as she moves from me to my daughters
to her mother to care for the ones
she brought into the world
& the one who brought her in too.
We stay steady
& safe, alive & whole.
A collective lineage of women.
Tied together
by her.

WHAT I WILL TO REMEMBER

Your small hands. Holding
toothbrushes & books. Out
to me & your father. The words
still labyrinth beneath
your fingers. Warm breath
at my shoulder. Damp hair
loose across my chest
the weight of all of you
& how it feels to see you slip
into sleep right before me.
Drowsy eyes & my own.
The heavy of my heart
to know you still need me
beside you.

TONIGHT—

I stay to lay eyes on them
feel their fingers in my hands,
warm their chilled cheeks,
swallow them in arms
with kisses to say
oh how I love you
oh how I've missed you
oh to see your small faces
keeping me still
warm. Protecting
me somehow
from all
the unknown
outside
our
door.

TODAY YOU ARE KITE

for Celi—age three

Tethered to anchor, you wail
through city sky—rambunctious free

fall, all orange & fuchsia, forget land
vault & anchor've got nothing

on your weightless wings—say
drag & wind, wind your way—

through fingers of five-year-olds
who know run & jaunt & hips thrown

to dance the dance of aerial funk
to bow & fight & force & inflate

in swaths of hemp & rayon & silk
& fragile-est of paper—cotton, come

on to altitude & resistance—cool
April wind, it's true all of you

is shape-shifter, super stunter
vast & fly   you are fly

fly

    fly.

MY MOTHER CALLS THEM MAGPIES—

& somehow the name fits. My daughters with full-on beaks
basking & flaunting on their walk/jaunt to school. First day
flitting & flirting in April's early sunshine. Each step, a float
from bodega to BX 36 bus stop. Their arms as wings, hailing

& Miriam, who caws, *Morning*, in a baritone. So the driver
says, *Hey there boss*. & they giggle incessant. *I'm a boss. No,
I'm a boss. We're both bosses. Are we bosses? Mom, mom,
mom, mom, mom, mommy, ma, mom, mooom, mama, ma*

their voices noisy, nonstop, a collective cacophonous chant
Yes, I say, insistent, persistent on my own. *Bird girl bosses, yes.*

ROOST

for Parneshia

Swear. It's not the high,
although we are. Stoned
& seventeen again. Guffaw
& caw from above.

Just one hit. & my old
peer-pressured ways sway
toward a yes. Downtown
Pacific Northwest. Legal

here. It's all pine trees
& fresh air. Us now city
kids aren't all the time
primed. So shock above

the slick black sheen
of one crow & then twelve
& then hundreds. Call it
a murder. & see the sky

boast a map of feathers,
beaks. A congregation
church of wings. Rowdy
rendezvous. Communal

shit. Streaming the streets
how we howl. Hold on to
each other. Say *isn't it all*
the time like this. A night

upturned with influx. Full
of flight & love, concrete
& haze. The sky above
migratory swarm of praise.

"LADY IN THE STREETS, BUT A FREAK IN THE BED"

Chris "Ludacris" Bridges

Nah. In the streets, watch me spit, suck, stuff, scrawl, loop, lilt, launch, lick—
out loud. Do deep squats at stoplights, & grind it loose while leaning
at the bus stop. I don't stop. Ride the pole on the A train, up & down, don't
give a thousand shits. You can witness. Or not. See my sexuality like a stable
of yeses trampling through your gut. I'm gut-wrenching. Wrecking all
the systems you create to tame me up, pose & poise me down to nothing.

& in the bed, by golly, I'm a buttoned-up, smoothed attitude having yes ma'am—
poised, cordial, crystal clear. I doggie style in a turtleneck if I please. Wear
big underwear that cover all my bottom if I wanna. Sip tea while you go down
on me. I'm proper, the exact equation of *if you please*, & *thank you for your
patience*. I'm etiquette-ed up. Use a lace napkin to wipe my mouth of your sex,
& the fancy china to serve myself on a gilded platter. All ladylike & cover-up.

How about this? I get to say who I am & how I want to be.

So I can be a freak whenever I wanna be. & a lady
whenever I very well please & thank you very much, sweetheart—wink. Stunt.

with all the women I love.
Rajeeyah & Lisa pose luminous
in front of neon lights. Glow
& strike. Lean. Renée & I light
up with laughter & we cackle
high & low. Nanya-Akuki
searches for the best dosas
spiced potatoes & chutney.
We study want & desire.
Decide on dinner while
searching the punk scene
& the start of stag films.
Tokumbo meets us after
& we trail toward Pongal.
Talk race & class & Beyoncé
& Toni Morrison & chakra
cards we read one by one
by one by one by one by one.
This sisterhood. Call us
all our names. Say love. See
us. Say trust & hope & laugh
& joy & much & miracle.
Yes. Say miracle. & see this.
These women. Surrounding
a table full of nourishment.
All of it. Such abundance yes.
Such luck to love this much.

HOW WE MAKE IT THROUGH

When you see Yesenia & Christina
in a crowded church turned poetry
project on St. Mark's in the village
full of rosé & words & deep sighs
at seeing faces you've not seen in so,
so long—you see family. How all of you
have grown community like. Some
flotation device cinching us all toward
one another. Elma's heart & everything
a circle can do. Cyclical. Cheryl
calling us to the page. Again. Again.
We write & heal & travel & make
babies & learn & listen & send
poems even when it's late & the kids
can't stop yelling & howling. Little
wolves who live in your living room.
& you're not sure you should have
ever entered another 30 poems
in 30 days. But here you are
still somehow above water. Breathing
real breath & alive. Cheers-ing
the rain-filled sky. & the women
who've made you. A home.

EACH DAY

Still new, this year is on fire.
& I am rocked in newsfeeds
from Jakarta to Victoria. A gulf
inside of me. Guzzle coffee,
cradle my anxiety with salt
& fat. Scroll the *Times*. Trauma
around every corner. My god.
How to get from one day
to the next.

But I think. There is this.
Miriam & Janella eating
happy meals consumed
in laughter & song.
Their voices small rafts
I hold strong to.
& dropping Celi at Sonja's
in Harlem the wind tears
through our coats,
but still. Still
there
is
this.

They are playing
Wonder Woman
& giggling relentless.
Such awe
at being 6.
& still their hearts.
& still the wind.
& still arms looped in a hug.
& still twirling.

& still the smallest kiss.
& still french fries.
& still breath.
& I am still
for once
all day.

FORTUNES

For Miriam—
It is very possible that you will achieve greatness in your lifetime

For Celi—
Many will travel to hear you speak

Their fortunes told
from sweet cookies
at Aquarius Seafood
off Main Street
Fort Lee calls
daily dim sum
rolled in carts
our way revolves
shrimp & pork
shu mai & dumplings
cold crisp cucumber
sautéed sliced beef
& we're savory
& divine Saturday
fine, fine, fine.

Their little lives
stretched wide spread
long & languid
before us, steaming
salt & pepper
calamari, curry chicken
eating the afternoon
how we lounge
in our appetites
long for futures
we can't see
don't even know
exist just yet.

I'M NOT DEAD, I'M DORMANT—

Not dead, kicking it. High gear.
Watch me meditate on my back,
you think I'm sleeping, checked
all the way out, but I'm blade
& bone & feathers & not here
for your fiction or your fantasy,
not your accessory or trophy, you
cannot polish me until I shine.
I'm already glowing without you.

You think you know my story
see me corpse pose & eyes closed
sometimes you can't see me
high tide, volcano, seawater, over
flow. But I'm here. I'm very much
breathing & sweating & wanting
& here, here, here, here, here, here.
Here.

BECAUSE

after Cheryl Boyce-Taylor

Because country, clay, dirt
& de-generate. Never been
known to de-escalate.
I'm a situation. 'Cause of cornbread
& don't I all the time say cornbread
as if anyone's forgotten my love.
Because bourbon, way a whole
town can get drunk on a mood.
Because Miriam Dawson Hagan
& Elinor Sferra Bazaz. 'Cause
Aziz & old family stories, poker
games round the table. New Haven
& Dumont, New Jersey,
rows of corn & fat tomatoes.
The flip-flops I lost down
the shore. Ocean. Floor & plankton,
Back woods & that good weed
highs & the creek-bed out back,
hush puppies we'd buy with quarters
pulled together. Hunger. Don't you
know I was wilder than you can even
imagine & I'm still loving. Living.
Can't read old journals without cringing.
Because Sterling & Old Barton's,
touring distilleries in grade school.
Born rowdy & rode it far & long
as I could. Because Aunt Tina
& cousins, cousins. Saltwater, sand
& cracking shrimp until they peel
straight from their bodies. Slick
& shining. New York Skyline. Because
I was 22 when I rode in on a yellow cab

from LGA with two suitcases & a whole
life I was leaving behind. Sometimes
you have to go far, far away
to ever come back home.

THE BALM—

Let me go on & gather all the nerve & all the ways
to say hurt & hold & ache. Let me deep sigh & meditate
on existence, ways to exist & bread. How to feed the crew
that shows up in my home ready to write & resist, dance,
dialogue, drink. Heal, figure out the steps, each move in all
directions. Let me open all my doors, arms & windows,
wave at the bus driver on Fort Washington who does not
under any circumstances drive the protesters to jail. Let them protest.

Endless. All hail, buy the books my kids need to be reading,
my students too, our shelves stuffed, and though I'm a pretty terrible cook
& no good in the kitchen, let me mix bourbon & water for those
who have been on their feet all day in the streets & in classrooms,
cold washcloth for your aching eyes from police brutality & violence
& pepper spray & violence & more violence, rub your feet for those
who have been on them for decades & decades. Let me listen, listen,
then speak up, then listen again, & be loud when it matters.

Clear the dance floor, BBQ picnic, bluegrass summer, tell folks
bring their whole selves & their mamaws & aunties to tell all the stories.
Don't forget the past & all that's been written & told about.
Let me get the porch swing & all the signs, let me celebrate with our classes
& art-making with artists I love. Let me not say I for the rest of this poem.

We should hold big celebrations, we should be big celebrations
showcasing young & old brilliance. Let us be like Lucille Clifton
& June Jordan & Nikky Finney & Naomi Shihab Nye & Alondra Uribe.
Go on & invite every damn one to the table, invest, be there
all of us home, a kind of home. Be this home—together.

WHAT TO DO

Pray. Or gnash your teeth.
Or steep the passion fruit
tea until your fingers stain.
Or laugh. Or build an altar.
Or become resource. Gold.
Or weep.

Or become blister, a blister
before it breaks. A blossom.
A gut of blood. Poison. Or run
a marathon of hawks into dust.
Or mount a deer, the limbs of each
past. Bend space. The distance.

Call everyone you know.
Or be grateful you were born
in the '70s. Anything to not obsess
over the fine indent in the middle
of your forehead that marks the days
& schedules, each one deeper. Each
crease of neck—a crepe, oh! God,
what comes next.

Knives are for steak, the tough meat
of some animal you can't cut through
with your teeth. Anyway, you never were
one to rely on beauty alone. The great big
Ha. & hell with sag & disaster. Hell with
skin you can't claim. Claim it anyway. Each
soft gray that plucks open from the top
of your skull like an alarm, something they'll tell you
to stop. Every chance they get. An advertisement
for better or more or smoother, or softer.

A breast to enhance, a stomach to staple,
skin to flush back, bones to rearrange, a whole
face to un-recognize—that even if you stunt it,
it still grows old, that even if it's pulled & hinged,
all hunched & singed, that even if it's plied
& pulled plump & filled in it still ages.
Bends & settles. Still prepares for the end.

Or the ever after anyway. Mood stabilizing.
A grain of self-contained, or what is a multitude
for how to chart existence, or why the hawk
always gets the rat—its teeth full of blood.
Why all the time what's hungry gets fed.
& vanity is voracious.

& you're tired of stuffing it full on itself.
Memorize the time it could take to be
this tender to who you are. How you're meant
to exist, be. Take it. Rest until your eyes glow.
Grow an orange grove in your lungs.
Love what comes next. & who you'll be
when the time arrives.

ACKNOWLEDGMENTS

The author thanks the editors of the following publications, in which some of the poems in this collection previously appeared.

Academy of American Poets: "Self-Portrait at 36 with David"

Birmingham Review: "Itemization," "Because"

Circe's Lament: Anthology of Wild Women Poetry, ed. Bianca Lynne Spriggs & Katerina Stoykova-Klemer (Accents Publishing, 2015): "Picture This"

Duende: "To Raise You, Daughter"

Miracle Monocle: "Search the Distance," "To both girls dipping bread in bowls of savory black beans in the Condesa—"

Moonshine, Two of Cups Press: "High Proof"

Pine Hills Review: "Miriam Dawson Hagan," "To Esmerely at Claire's, who tells my daughters it won't hurt—"

Poetry Northwest: "To the hawk that circled J. Hood Park—" and "To the sleeping woman in Cindy's bakery on the corner of St. Nicholas & 179th St."

Scalawag: "Miriam"

Solstice Literary Magazine: "Lady in the streets, but a freak in the bed," "My mother calls them magpies—"

Split This Rock: "What We Do—Now"

Women of Resistance: Poems for a New Feminism, ed. Danielle Barnhart & Iris Mahan (OR Books, 2018): "To the breasts when it's over,—" and "To the woman on St. Nicholas Avenue whose thigh was a wilderness blooming—"

Always thankful for the friends & artists who ride & dance & sing & love beside me in this wild world. Forever grateful for: Grisel Y. Acosta, Juan Acosta, Stephanie Dionne Acosta, Olivia Aguilar, Lisa Ascalon, Jennifer Baker, Julia Berick, Dan Bernitt, Berry, Leslie Hibbs Blincoe, Tokumbo Bodunde, Marc Boone, Lori Brown-Niang, Susan Buttenwieser, Moriah Carlson, Becca Christensen, Olivia Cole, Bobby DeJesus, Jessica Diaz, Mitchell L. H. Douglas, Jason Duchin, Dana Edell, Kelly Norman Ellis, John Ellrodt, Maria Fico, Rajeeyah Finnie-Myers, D. A. Flores, Kevin Flores, Marsha Flores, Asha French, Tanya Gallo, Catrina Ganey, Megan Clark Garriga, Anne Gendler, Nanya-Akuki Goodrich, Rachel Eliza Griffiths, Andrée Greene, Lisa Green,

Ysabel Y. Gonzalez, Jake Hagan, Jen Hagan, Michael Hagan, Lisa Hagan, Karen Harryman, Lindsey Homra, Marianne Jankowski, Melissa Johnson, Amanda Johnston, Carey Kasten, Caroline Kennedy, Michele Kotler, Britt Kulsveen, Rob Linné, Veronica Liu, Mino Lora, Tim Lord, Will Maloney, Alison McDonald, Stacy Mohammed, Kamilah Aisha Moon, Andrea Murphy, Willie Perdomo, Andy Powell, Sarina Prabasi, Danni Quintos, David Reilly, Carla Repice, Brandi Cusick Rimpsey, Lisa Forsee Roby, Kate Dworkoski Scudese, Pete Scudese, Melanie Ballard Sewell, Kate Carothers Smith, Anne Tappan Strother, Vincent Toro, Natalia Torres, Alondra Uribe, Jessica Wahlstrom, Renée Watson, Kelly Wheatley, Crystal Wilkinson, and Marina Hope Wilson.

Elma's Heart Circle & all the women who are a home for me. Cheryl Boyce-Taylor especially & always, & this stunning sisterhood of poets: E. J. Antonio, Cheryl Clarke, LeConté Dill, Kathy Engel, JP Howard, Caits Meissner, Yesenia Montilla & Christina Olivares.

Aracelis Girmay for your friendship & vision & clarity & conversations & for seeing this work. Thank you always & love.

Parneshia Jones for your brilliance & heart & sharp, sharp editorial eye. & for the entire team at Northwestern for caring so deeply for the work & sharing it with the world.

For the family collectives of the following: Affrilachian Poets, Alice Hoffman Young Writers Retreat at Adelphi University, Café Buunni, Conjwoman, the DreamYard Project, Geraldine R. Dodge Poetry Festival, girlstory, GlobalWrites, International Poetry Exchange Program, Kentucky Governor's School for the Arts, Northern Manhattan Arts Alliance, Northwestern University Press, People's Theatre Project, Rad(ical) Poetry Consortium, Sawyer House Press, VONA: The Voices of our Nations Arts Foundation & Word Up Community Bookshop/Libreria Comunitaria.

For my parents—always. Gianina & Patrick Hagan for always celebrating & nurturing the artist side of me. I love, love you both.

For my love—David Flores. You are all & everything to me. What luck to love this much.

Finally to my daughters—my whole, whole hearts. So much love to you both. Araceli Miriam Hagan Flores & Miriam Elinor Hagan Flores. You two are anchor & blessing. Love, always.